Creative Thought

Making it Happen

By

David Ross

Ersatz Publishing

Copyright 2008 by David Ross All rights reserved
ISBN: 978-0-6151-8799-0
First Ersatz Publishing printing: January, 2008
Ersatz Publishing

www.ersatz.com

PO Box 862
Lake Arrowhead, CA 92352
davidross@izotz.com

CREATIVE THOUGHT IS A PROCESS

IT MUST PRODUCE SOMETHING OF TANGIBLE VALUE

IT REQUIRES CONSCIOUS EFFORT

SET THE PHYSICAL STAGE

SET THE PSYCHOLOGICAL STAGE

DEFINE THE PROBLEM

FIND THE ESSENCE OF THE PROBLEM

THINK CREATIVE THOUGHTS

WHEN NECESSARY, STEP BACK AND CHANGE PERSPECTIVE

KNOW WHEN TO STOP

GET ON WITH IT

Preface

I wrote this for myself, as a self-help book. I'm a professional creative thinker, and sometimes I need help doing my job. I've been doing creative thinking for more than thirty years, and over that time I've cobbled together a collection of thoughts about the process, some of which have ended up on notes taped to the wall in my workspace to be read whenever I get stuck while doing it. Inspirational thoughts for making creative thinking happen. Sometimes they help. So I collected all those notes, added some words, and put them into this book. Now, whenever I get stuck, I open this up, review what's worked in the past, and usually can find a way forward. If you should find yourself in possession of this book, and discover anything of value in it, then all the effort I made to assemble these thoughts, format the text, and spell check the words will be doubly worthwhile. In any case, it sometimes sure helps me a whole lot.

Contents

*Conditions for creativity are to be
puzzled; to concentrate; to accept conflict
and tension; to be born every day; to feel
a sense of self.*

-Erick Fromm

Creative Thought

I get paid to think creative thoughts. I've been getting paid to do this for a long time. First as an architect, then as an artist, then as a software designer, then as a cartoonist, and most recently as a writer – it is my vocation. I've had to figure out how to make creative thoughts happen regular enough to get people to pay me money so I could pay the rent. You don't last very long as creative thinker if you don't have enough creative thoughts. Along the way I discovered that it didn't matter what job I was doing, the process of creative thought always seemed to be the same.

This book will tell you about what I've learned about doing professional creative thinking. I love the creative process, and can't imagine a more fun and exciting job.

Thought Processing

I am a *Thought Processor*. I take *creative thoughts* and *process* them into things of *tangible value*. Many people do this every day as they work their jobs and live out their lives, but for the most part they do it subconsciously and often by accident. A *professional thought processor* can't afford to depend on the occasional happy accident to provide a consistent stream of tangible results – their creative thought process must be deliberate, reliable, and available on demand. It needs to be predictable – and produce successful results more often than it does not.

Can creative thought be predictable and controllable? Some creative thinkers depend entirely on the happenstance of unforeseen *EUREKA!* moments, placing total faith in the pure magic of the creative act. Others, more dependent on producing regular results of tangible value, have learned that there are things you can do to increase the odds that creative thought can indeed be a deliberate and conscious act more reliable and predictable than waiting – and hoping – for lightning to strike. This book is about learning what you can do to help kick start creative thought and turn it into a conscious process that results in predictable results on a regular basis. It will help you become a *thought processor.*

Who Needs Creative Thought?

Architects, artists, musicians, doctors, lawyers, writers, parents, teachers, students, firemen, policemen, soldiers, politicians, mothers, fathers, children – pretty much all of us. Some people use it on a daily basis while others need it only occasionally, but just about everyone can use creative thought to overcome obstacles, pursue opportunity, or solve problems every now and then. Some of us need to use creative thought every day – it pays the rent.

Everyone is a genius at least once a year.
A real genius has his original ideas closer
together.

-George Lichtenberg

You Think, Therefore You Can Create

Creative thinking is both a *skill* and a *talent*. Without creative thinking skills, talent likely remains underused, or worse, ignored completely. Depending on what story you choose to believe, some suggest that creative talent comes from DNA inherited from a creative parent or grandparent, or bestowed by some omnipotent spiritual being, or because of fateful blind luck in the way your genes came together – and there isn't much anyone can do to help you become a creative thinker. But know this – if you can think – you can have creative thoughts. If you can have creative thoughts, you can *learn* skills to help you have creative thoughts more often. Being that every human I know can think, this means that if you take some time to learn thinking skills, your ability to have more and better creative thoughts can improve dramatically.

What is Creative Thought?

Creative thought is a *process*. The goal of the process is to produce something of *tangible value* – such as the solution to a problem, a new work of art, or an idea that provides financial opportunity. It is a *conscious* process – triggered by the need to solve a problem or make a discovery.

This process can take seconds, hours, days, or sometimes many frustrating years of effort. Along the way you never know what will come of it – sometimes nothing, sometimes fame and glory. Usually it's something mundane like a pat on the back and *"here's your next job."* But that's okay. For many of us the uncertainty contains the seed of great joy – *the joy of discovery* – the most personal of the tangible results offered by successful completion of the creative thought process. And if you end up creating something useful and earn great riches and fame, so much the better.

You can never solve a problem on the level on which it was created.

-Albert Einstein

Creativity is a type of learning process where the teacher and pupil are located in the same individual.

-Arthur Koestler

Setting Up For Creative Thought

Setting the Stage

Effective creative thought almost always requires *conscious* effort. Sometimes you get lucky and effortless magic just happens, but usually people need to consciously set the stage and create an environment conducive to *making* it happen. If there is one misconception about creative thinkers that lay people seem to hold above all others – it's that *creative people seem to do what they do without trying* - effortlessly. Nothing could be more wrong. Creative thought requires conscious effort – one which begins with *setting the stage*. I've been a thought processor for a long time, yet I still have to step back and consciously kick myself into creative thought mode almost every time I set out on a quest.

Setting the stage for creative thought means *creating the ideal physical and psychological environment most conducive to provoking creative thinking*. This *ideal* environment may vary significantly between individuals. It can also vary significantly for an individual himself depending on what he's been asked to do, time frame, mood of the moment, and a variety of other conditions. But most people who routinely do creative work discover a specific set of physical and psychological circumstances that seem to inspire creative thought, and have become adept at recreating those circumstances on demand.

Setting the Physical Stage

Most people already know when and where it is that they "do their best thinking". For some, it's early in the morning or late at night when everyone else is in bed and the phone has stopped ringing. For others it can be the middle part of the day after the mind has fully woken up but before growing tired in the late afternoon. Some people need the peace and quiet of an extended walk on a wooded trail, and others turn on while seated in a noisy meeting room filled with collaborators. The first step in learning to set the stage is to *consciously* recognize what kinds of physical environments *work best* for you – not just work – but *work best*. Everyone can "think" anywhere, but what do you need to think *best?*

Once identified, it becomes your job to set the stage by *consciously* creating that environment whenever you embark on a creative thought project. Painters can't paint unless they have good brushes and a quiet room, musicians can't make good music without instruments and a place they can make a lot of noise, and you aren't going to do *your* best thinking unless you are in an environment conducive to creative thought. This isn't always easy to do. You might have a boss who doesn't understand the concept of a long walk through nature, and instead needs to see you sitting in your cubicle punching the keyboard. Your spouse and kids don't understand the meaning of quiet time. The dog needs walking and that darn phone won't stop ringing. But know this – *if you can't set the stage, you won't be doing much creative thought. You must find a way to do it.* If you are a professional thought processor, you must find a way to do it on demand. *That's part of the job – to consciously set the stage for creative thinking.*

Using Multiple Stages

Some people only need to exercise creative thought on an irregular basis. For them, finding a *single* technique they can use to provoke creative thought might suffice. Maybe all it takes is a long walk on a nature trail, a drive in the country, or to sit on the edge of a pretty lake for a couple hours.

But if you are a professional thought processor, you need to find a way to set the stage on a regular and predictable schedule in a way that accommodates the varying requirements of the specific job at hand. This means you will need *multiple stages* to choose from. Some stage environments work best for short projects and some work better for long ones. Some will be financially cheaper and some will be very expensive. Some work better in the summer. If you decide that the only way you can do your best creative thinking is to take long walks in the balmy evenings along the shoreline on a tropical island, you are going to have a problem sustaining a career as a professional thought processor – unless you happen to live full time next to the beach on a tropical island. It rains, it snows, you might be someplace where taking a walk could get you mugged, you don't have an expense account – you aren't always going to be walking down that beach. You need flexible alternatives.

Part of your job as a thought processor is to identify multiple physical environments that will work to promote creative thought. *You need to be able to perform on multiple stages.*

Building the Stage

Some people can sit down wherever they happen to be at the moment, flip a mental switch, and pump out creative thoughts all day long. But most of us need to do a little bit more to set the stage environment for ourselves. Exactly *what* we need to do depends on what our own stage is supposed to look like. And to figure that out, we need to know what scenery needs to be included on the stage. Do you need peace and quiet? Do you need to be free from distraction? Do you need a place to get out and walk? These are the vital components that you'll assemble into a stage environment.

The scenery that makes up your own stage environment is not just an abstract concept. It consists of tangible components, and can be broken down into a list of specific requirements. Figuring out those specific requirements is something of a creative act unto itself, and to do it you might want to make use of a technique called "*Finding the Essence*", which we'll talk about in chapter 7.

You probably already know under what conditions you can do your best creative thinking, or at least you've got some inkling because you've had success in the past under certain conditions. Sit down and think carefully about those times. What you want to do is identify in simplest terms the fundamental characteristics of the environment that promoted successful creative thinking. You need to strip those characteristics down to the bone and *"find the essence"* of what it was that made it work for you. Were you alone? Was it quiet? Was the phone turned off? Were you secure from interruption? Did you have minimal distraction? All these fundamental characteristics should go on your list. Then, when you've got it all down...rank everything in terms of importance. When you are done, you should have an ordered list of maybe ten or fifteen environmental characteristics that make it easier for you to do creative thinking. More than fifteen and you are being too specific. Less than ten and you are either really easy to please, or you aren't defining the true essence of the environment.

Once you've done this, you can effectively set the stage for creative thought by using your list of required characteristics to build an environment that works for you. Shuffle the list to come up with multiple stages. Remember what I said about needing multiple stages? Your list will tell you what you need – use a little creative thought (!) and put it all together into different stage environments.

At first you should carry your list around with you, and look it over each time you embark on a creative thought project. If you are having problems performing, check your list and see if maybe you haven't set up your environment properly. I know it sounds stupid and simple, but it's actually pretty easy to forget that all your best ideas come during long walks or whatever, and here you sit in a cubicle staring at a computer screen trying to create magic. GET OUT AND WALK! Eventually you'll memorize the whole routine well enough that maybe you think you won't need a written list when building your stage. I keep mine around, because whenever I get hung up and feel uncreative, a quick review sometimes clues me into a change I should make in my environment, or highlights a different approach that might break my deadlock.

Building Blocks

Here are a few of the building blocks that commonly show up on the lists of people who have been doing thought processing for a long time. You'll notice that most of these things directly attack the Big Two Impediments to Creative Thought – *distraction* and *negative state of mind*.

Disconnect the Distraction – Nothing derails the creative train faster than distraction. Get something going – next thing you know someone wants to tell you all about a television show from last night or a personal crisis or a funny joke. Few people can completely eliminate distraction, and even if you tried, there will always be unpredictable distractions sneaking up on you despite your best efforts to sequester yourself on the metaphorical moon. Instead, the thing you need to do is *control* distraction the best you can. Turn on the answer machine and screen calls. Tell people you don't want to be disturbed. Lock your door. The goal is to minimize the potential for distraction, and reduce the disruption when it occurs. *Disconnect the distraction.*

Block out the time – Some people claim they do their best work under a tight deadline. That might be true, but "tight" doesn't mean "unrealistic". If you don't have enough time to finish a project, you'll probably end up spending a significant amount of your creative thought thinking about how fast that clock is moving. Knowing how much time to allow yourself to come up with the creative solution to a problem is never easy. It's not like mowing the yard – you can't simply do a few test passes, multiply by the size of the yard, and come up with a fairly accurate idea of when you'll be done. Experienced thought processors can sometimes come up with some idea of how long a particular project might take – especially if it's something similar to what they've done before – but beginning thought processors are usually best served by trying to block out the largest reasonable chunk of time possible, with maybe a backup plan just in case. You'll find that as you get better at setting the stage your performance becomes more predictable, and your time estimates become more accurate. After all, that's the whole point of approaching the creative thought process in a deliberate and conscious manner – to make it more predictable.

Exercising the body exercises the mind – Sure, it sounds hokey. But it works. Exercise clears the mind and stimulates release of various chemicals in your body that help your brain work better. Try to find something you can physically do for an hour or more that isn't of real high intensity. Sometimes all it takes is a five minute walk around the parking lot, but more often you need some time to let your mind get into the swing of it. Walking is a great low intensity exercise that doesn't require a lot of focus and doesn't leave you so winded that all you can think about is *"when is this going to end?"* If it's snowing outside, maybe find a treadmill. Be sure to carry a notepad and pen for when creative thought start kicking in. If you're the kind of person who likes to talk to themselves out loud, take one of those digital recorder things. You don't want to forget anything that comes up during your walk.

Quiet please – It's probably fairly obvious that most people think best when they are in a relatively quiet environment. Some people thrive on the stimulation afforded by noisy crowds, but for most of us noise equals distraction. Find your own balance. The goal is to get to a place where you don't have to spend mental energy overcoming the distracting noise going on around you.

Maintain your momentum – Make sure you can sustain your stage environment long enough to finish the job. Few things are more frustrating – or more counterproductive – than to find yourself deep in good creative thought but interrupted by distraction, especially when it was a predictable distraction. Momentum is one of the hardest things to create. Protect it.

Change of scenery – Go somewhere different or go to some special place you've set aside to do creative thinking. Unusual settings often provoke creative thinking. Unfortunately for corporate America, a noisy shared cubicle surrounded by short partitions, ringing telephones, and coworkers who insist on telling the latest joke whenever they feel like it isn't likely to put someone in the right frame of mind to think creative thoughts. This does *not* mean you have to go to Tahiti. Maybe it just means you go sit out on the lawn in front of your office building, or up on the roof, or to a nearby park. In fact, there is a real downside to going somewhere *too* new and dramatic. Walking around Yosemite isn't likely to stimulate much creative thought. Remember, it's all about disconnecting the distraction…and looking up at fresh snow on Half Dome on a spectacular fall day is definitely going to be a distraction. Go somewhere different and special, but not so different that you spend all your time gawking at the scenery.

Timely breaks – Give yourself a break. Stop thinking for a few moments. Do something different. Many people find that a break can *trigger* a flood of creative thoughts – especially when stuck in a rut. Spinning your wheels rarely gets you out of a rut, and in fact may just bury you deeper. Get out of the car and take a short walk. When you get back you may just suddenly see that big log you can shove under your tire – and get yourself out.

Access to Technology – Make sure you have everything you need. Seems self evident, but how many times have you checked into a motel promising "High Speed Internet" and found out it wasn't. If you depend on high speed internet, you'll have an awful problem. Whatever you need – pencil and plenty of paper, a cell connection, crayons – make sure you have it. Spending time tracking down a power cord for your laptop is not only a distraction, but it will likely put you into an uncreative state of mind. Especially if you are in an unfamiliar town and have to spend two hours searching for that Radio Shack "just down the street". Stock your pantry before you start.

Collaboration – Do you need to surround yourself with a crowd of like-minded people all pursuing a unified creative goal? If so, the stage needs to be set for the entire group. Collaboration is a critical and necessary part of many creative projects. Sometimes you need to collaborate with a single person – in which case you should make sure that person is available during your creative thought project – and sometimes you need to collaborate with an entire group of people thrown together in a conference room. Make sure everything possible has been done to set the stage for the entire group. Group collaborations aren't much different than solo efforts. The same basic building blocks are used to create a physical and psychological group environment conducive to provoking creative thought.

Set aside your problems – This is not the time to be thinking about your financial problems. Nor is it the time to resolve your relationship issues. Nor is it the time to plan your wedding, call your bookie, or worry about losing your hair. Disconnect the distractions, at least for a while.

Figure out where you're going to eat – Seems like an irrelevant thing – something we all do every day without much fuss or muss. But remember, setting the stage is all about reducing potential distractions and setting up positive state of mind. Not having access to the right food, at the right times, and in the right setting will not only be a huge distraction as you try to get yourself fed, but an improperly nourished human mind can be very unproductive, and usually is not in a very creative state. It's pretty hard to think good creative thoughts when you are hungry and cranky from the lack of food.

Chemical inspiration – Some people swear they do their best work while suspended in a chemically inspired state of creative utopia. Whether it's via alcohol or one of the other many chemical concoctions available to anyone so inclined, they contend such an altered state of being inspires great thinking. I know that it sometimes works for me. The problem is, when it wears off, I usually can't remember what I did, and if I've somehow managed to write it all down during the experience, it comes out looking like the writings of an inebriated fool. Most creative thinkers figure out early on that while chemical inspiration may occasionally produce some kind of *EUREKA!* moment worthy of the inevitable painful recovery process, doing it on a regular basis is a short straight road to ruin. If you depend on chemical inspiration to set the stage, your career probably won't last very long, and you won't consistently produce good work. The side of the road is littered with the bones of those who've tried.

The problem is never how to get new, innovative thoughts into your mind, but how to get old ones out. Every mind is a building filled with archaic furniture. Clean out a corner of your mind and creativity will instantly fill it.

-Dee Hock

Setting the Psychological Stage

In addition to setting the physical stage, you also need to set the psychological stage. Setting the physical stage determines when and where you will do creative thought. Setting the psychological stage puts you in the right *frame of mind* to do it. You need to consciously create the right frame of mind in which creative thought is most likely to occur.

Look at the list of environmental requirements described in the previous chapter and note that the real end goal for most of them is to exert control over things that may negatively impact your state of mind and to limit distraction. Reducing distraction has a significant psychological effect because not only does it leave your mind empty enough for creative thinking to occur, but by reducing the aggravation caused by unwanted distractions it leaves you in a better frame of mind to think positively about things. Many people consider a positive state of mind to be an important prerequisite for creative thinking.

The Quiet Mind

Only a lucky few can be creative while their mind is distracted by thoughts of the overdue phone bill or the car that needs new tires or the doctor appointment or whether it will snow or not. Most people know that they do their best thinking only after they set aside such distractions and allow their thoughts to focus in on the task at hand. Why? Because by setting aside distractions, they've allowed their mind to quiet down. **A *quiet mind* stimulates creative thought.**

Most professional thought processors are familiar with the idea of the *quiet mind.* In one form or another the concept is usually taught in design schools, self improvement programs, and other programs where the ultimate goal is to help people be more productive in their thinking. Rightly so, *because the concept of the Quiet Mind is probably the one most powerful and effective tool available to the creative thinker.*

The idea behind the *quiet mind* is that by reducing the mental clutter and distraction that surrounds daily existence, we give our mind the breathing room it needs to function effectively and produce creative thinking. It's a very simple and obvious concept, and few people would argue with the validity of the idea. Most people probably already have plenty of experience in how well it works – even if they've never given it a name. The reason we want to actually *name* the concept – and to define it – is so that we can begin to *use it in a conscious and purposeful manner during the creative thought process.* In other words, rather than relying on happenstance to produce the kind of quiet mind most conducive to producing creative thought – we want to be able to call it up on demand and make it a routine part of setting the psychological stage.

The concept of the *quiet mind* is easy to understand. Most people can readily accept the idea that you think better if you aren't distracted by the minutia of daily life. Learning to create the quiet mind on demand really isn't much more difficult than understanding the concept itself. It does take conscious effort, and it will take practice to get to where you can almost always call it up, but the method is pretty simple.

There is a technique that Zen aficionados use while they meditate – it's called the *empty mind.* While the purpose of Zen meditation (*to become still and empty*) is different than your goal (*to do creative thinking*), how you achieve the Zen empty mind using meditation techniques can also be used to create a quiet mind suitable for doing creative thinking. In a nutshell: while meditating, most people will pass through a state of peaceful quietness where the random noise generated by mental distraction has decreased to the point where creative thought begins to occur – they've created a *quiet* mind. The goal of Zen meditation is to take you further than that – all the way to an *empty* mind. But for our purposes, a *quiet mind* is what we want. Fortunately, since most of us have neither the aptitude nor time to properly perform Zen meditation on a regular basis, what we can do is take one of the simplest of meditation techniques and use it for our own purposes in the effort to create a quiet mind.

Zen masters teach you that the trick to reaching the desired empty mind is to learn how to *not **hang onto** thoughts as they pass in and out of your mind during the meditative process.* If you sit quietly for a few minutes and consciously track what thoughts pass through your mind, you'll find that you probably think randomly about a whole host of different things – maybe about money or people or things or sports or food – and that each one of these thoughts can easily take on a life of its own and monopolize your mind for a few seconds, minutes, or even hours. If your goal is to reach a state of empty mind, such random thoughts don't help you very much. So in Zen they'll teach you to learn how to let those random thoughts slip *out* of your mind just as quickly as they slip in. Don't *hang onto* your thoughts – let them slip away. You can't really just turn off your mind – it's always thinking – but if you can learn to control the flow of thoughts better, you can learn to attain a state of empty mind, and, you can also learn to create a quiet mind. For our purposes, learning how to allow unwanted thoughts to easily pass out of mind allows the desired creative thinking process to more readily occur. And luckily for us, this technique doesn't require a lot of time or a meditation mat or a quiet environment – you can use it anywhere, anytime.

Learning to let go of distracting thoughts is a key technique used in creating a quiet mind. When you think about it, many of the other things you do while setting a physical or psychological stage also contribute to a quiet mind. Choosing your environment, turning off the phone, arranging meals – all of this reduces the potential for distraction. Distraction is the hobgoblin of a quiet mind.

Learning to create a quiet mind is one of the most useful things you can do to set the psychological stage for creative thought.

Be *Flexible*...Don't Shoot Yourself in the Foot

The whole reason you went through the process of creating a list of required characteristics for your stage environment was so that you could take those individual requirements, juggle them around, and combine them into *multiple* stage configurations whenever necessary. Be flexible – don't get trapped by *"I can only work if I have complete quiet, total isolation and inspirational scenery"*. As said earlier, most people need to develop multiple stages; few of us can always work from a single stage. So be creative. Try different things. You never know when you'll stumble onto a better and more productive way of provoking creative thought.

Remember most of all that setting the stage for creative thought requires a *conscious* effort on *your* part. It won't just happen, and nobody is going to do it for you. Setting the stage is a skill that you need to develop and use every time you embark on a creative thought project.

Don't set yourself up for failure. You can't use the lack of a stage as an excuse for nonperformance. *Find a way to set the stage.* It's your job to do *whatever it takes* to set the physical stage for creative thought. No excuses allowed. That's your job.

It is better to have enough ideas for some of them to be wrong, than to be always right by having no ideas at all.

-Edward De Bono

The best way to have a good idea is to have lots of ideas.

-Linus Pauling

All children are artists. The problem is how to remain an artist once he grows up.

-Pablo Picasso

Creativity is the ability to see relationships where none exist.

-Thomas Disch

Making the simple complicated is commonplace; making the complicated simple, awesomely simple, that's creativity.

-Charles Mingus

When I am working on a problem I never think about beauty. I only think about how to solve the problem. But when I have finished, if the solution is not beautiful, I know it is wrong.

-Buckminster Fuller

Doing Creative Thinking

The Stage is Set – Now What?

So you've set the stage and put yourself into a quiet state of mind – the creative thoughts will just come pouring out – right? Maybe if you're lucky, but usually not. You've still got to make *conscious effort*.

Solving a Problem

Usually when you start the creative thought process you have a goal. Maybe you are trying to solve some problem. Maybe you are trying to figure out some way to pursue an opportunity – or create one. Maybe you are trying to come up with some new software, or a book plot, or a piece of music, or fix some personal issue. Whatever that goal may be, think of it as *The Problem* – and you are trying to solve it.

Define the Problem

Before you can solve a problem, you have to know what it is. If you don't know what the problem is, you'll never know when you've solved it.

Finding the Essence

Defining the problem is the most critical, important, and useful action you can take when it comes to successfully completing your creative thought task. The key to properly defining the problem is ***finding its essence*** – stripping away the unnecessary, irrelevant, and unimportant to find the intrinsic, indispensable, and crucial properties that *characterize the true nature* of what it is you are trying to accomplish.

Once you think you've come up with a definition, express the essence of the problem in twenty five words or less. If you can't do that, you haven't found the true essence. Reduce it further until you can.

The Mission Statement

This definition becomes the project *Mission Statement – the essence of the problem* – and will be used throughout the creative thought process to not only help you come up with potential solutions, but equally important *evaluate* those solutions to make sure you've stayed true to the desired goal. Without an adequate and accurate definition of the problem, you'll never know whether or not you've actually solved it.

Defining the problem is an act of creative thought in itself. Sometimes it's easy to do, but often can be the most difficult part of the creative process. Nothing in the creative thought process is more important. *Lack of an adequate and accurate definition will lead to fuzzy thinking, which will lead to fuzzy solutions, which will lead to at best mediocre solutions, and at worst complete failure at whatever it was you set out to do.* **Find the essence and define the problem. Success depends on it.**

Creative Thinking Tactics

The stage is set, your mind is right, and you've defined the problem. Now – *Let It Happen*. Following are some tactics you can use to encourage creative thought. Any of these can kick start your creative thought process, or even better, rescue it should you run up against the proverbial brick wall.

Looking for Ideas – Inspiration

You collect ideas every minute you breathe. Everything you see, dream, read, feel, hear, and touch accumulates in the file cabinet you call your brain in a disorganized freeform collection of disparate thoughts piled willy-nilly together without discernable structure. So go rummaging. Open your eyes and your mind. Free associate seemingly unrelated thoughts. Mine metaphorical comparisons – the structure of a tree; the ripple of waves; the ordered flow of cars on a freeway – do any of these things apply to your problem? Get historical – does anything in your past resemble the current problem? Does anything in the history of the world resemble the current problem?

Shuffle the Deck

Take all your thoughts and shuffle them up. Pair them in different ways. Reorder them. Eliminate some. Add some. Re-deal. Maybe putting "B" before "A" illuminates the solution, or at least sheds an interesting new light on the problem, leading to further explorations. Just because you've had a few good thoughts, don't get trapped by partial success. Shuffle the deck and see what comes out.

Change Your Perspective

All artists know about looking at their artwork upside down and backwards. They stand bent over looking at the canvas through their legs. No, they aren't crazy – it's the quickest way to see errors in balance, proportion, and color. Why? Because it gives them a different perspective. If you stand and stare long enough at something – such as when you painstakingly paint a landscape – it always seems "right". Look at it backwards, and suddenly you see it isn't. Step back, step sideways, step above, turn it upside down. Figure out how to look at your problem from a different perspective.

Set Aside All that You Know.

Beware the *knowledgeable expert* trap. It's an ironic truth that quite often the more knowledgeable you are in a field, the harder it becomes to some up with innovation and creative solutions. Why? Because as "experts" we find ourselves following familiar pathways looking to short circuit the search. After all, being an expert in the field, you should be able to come up with something spectacular simply because you know so much. Unfortunately, all that knowledge can stand in the way of new and creative thinking, blinding you to new and fresh ideas. Avoid the trap. Step back, set aside what you know – enlist others (with less expertise) to help you see things fresh – don't get trapped by your expertness.

Verify the Definition

If you find yourself stuck, go back and make sure that you've accurately and adequately defined the essence of the problem – that your mission statement is a good one. Many "brick walls" are in fact nothing more than an ill-defined problem.

Redefine the Problem

If you *really* find yourself stuck, redefine the problem. You can't get anywhere on a dead end road.

Derivative Thinking

Don't confuse *creative thought* with *original thought*. The fact is, coming up with a truly *original* thought is extremely difficult to do, and most of us – while we may be successful creative thinkers –

will go our whole lives without ever coming up with something truly original. Nor is it usually necessary. Remember, your job is to *solve the problem.* Unless something in the definition of your problem requires that the solution be something truly *original* – and that's something that doesn't happen very often – your focus should be on coming up with the *best* possible solution, irregardless of whether it's an *original* solution. Most successful creative thinkers work derivatively – that is they build on the thinking of others, adapting successful solutions to their own problems. Like the old saying goes – *there's no sense reinventing the wheel if you don't have to.* The wheel is a pretty clever invention, and trying to come up with something original – when a simple wheel would solve the problem at hand just fine – will most likely just send you down a bumpy road that will most likely just end in a dead end. The funny thing is, if you are a successful *creative* thinker – meaning you succeed in solving problems more often than not – you'll also be perceived as an *original* thinker. Most people don't know the difference. In the end all that really matters is that you successfully solve the problem at hand. Along the way if you come up with some truly original thought, bully for you.

Think Outside the Box

As overused as the saying is, it's still true that *thinking outside the box* quite often leads to creative solutions. Doing some of the things listed above – changing perspective, shuffling the deck, setting aside all you know, redefining the problem – are common techniques that help you think outside the box. Do those things, but also step back and consciously vocalize the idea that "now I'm going to think outside the box". Make it a conscious effort.

Managing Fear and Doubt

Fear and doubt plague all creative thinkers. Everyone goes through periods where they think they've "lost the magic" – where nothing seems to work, where the challenge seems overwhelming. Sometimes these periods last years, sometimes they last minutes. They can occur randomly, and sometimes happen just when you're on a roll and end up bringing your creative thought process to a screeching dead halt. It's no fun when it happens, and can challenge even the most confident among us. The thing you have to know is this – *fear and doubt are an integral part of the creative process.* It comes with the territory. It's a part of the job. Few entirely avoid it. Most importantly, you have to know that it goes away – even more importantly – you can make it go away. Fear and doubt will paralyze you if you let it. Don't let it. Everything you've read up to this point can be used to help overcome fear and doubt – to spark forward movement – and to move you towards a successful conclusion. If you find yourself paralyzed by fear and/or doubt, take a few steps back, shuffle the deck, reread the definition of the problem, change to a different stage, take a break – whatever it takes – overcoming fear and doubt is a part of the job. You have the tools to do it, but it takes effort and conscious thought.

Getting Tangible Results

Remember, the goal of creative thought is to produce something of *tangible* value. If you don't end up producing a tangible result, all you've done is kill time. Killing time doing creative thinking may be amusing and entertaining, but it serves no practical purpose. If your goal is to be a professional thought processor, it's unlikely that you'll ever get anyone to pay you to just kill time. If your goal is to solve some concrete problem, failing to find a tangible result means you don't solve the problem.

Therefore, a critical and necessary part of the creative process is *getting a tangible result.*

Learning When to Stop…GET ON WITH IT!

The interesting thing about the creative process is that if you've done everything you're supposed to do – setting the stage, getting your mind right, making conscious and sustained effort at doing the creative thinking – you've probably successfully come up with a tangible result. In other words, you've *solved the problem.* Now the issue isn't that you've failed to do so – the more likely thing is that you've failed to *recognize* that you've done it. One of the hardest lessons for artists to learn is *when to put down the brush.* Creative thinkers suffer the same affliction – whether they simply enjoy the process too much and don't want it to stop, or don't know how to recognize the solution when it appears – knowing when to stop is a crucial part of the creative process. This is one reason why it's so important to *define the essence of the problem* at the beginning of the process – because you need to be able to recognize that the job is done when it's done, that it's good

enough, and that it's *TIME TO GET ON WITH IT*. That means —
it's time to stop thinking and implement your solution. *Pay attention
to what you are doing during the creative thought process, keep reviewing your
definition of the problem, and learn to recognize when you're done.*

The moment when you first wake up in the morning is the most wonderful of the twenty-four hours. No matter how weary or dreary you may feel, you possess the certainty that, during the day that lies before you, absolutely anything may happen. And the fact that it practically always doesn't, matters not a jot. The possibility is always there.

-Monica Baldwin

Happiness is not in the mere possession of money; it lies in the joy of achievement, in the thrill of creative effort.

-Franklin D. Roosevelt

Creative Thought

Creative thought – and the creative process in general – is for many people one of the most exciting adventures they can ever imagine doing. The intellectual challenge; the chance to think up exciting things; the thrill of discovery – are all facets of the rewarding life of the *thought processor.* For many people, the specifics of what they do are irrelevant – just to be doing creative thinking is often enough. That's why you hear of so many creative thinkers who end up in multiple careers. The thrill of the creative process leads them down all kinds of interesting roads.

If this book has given you even one small insight – and possibly even helped you in some small way or sparked an enthusiasm for the creative thought process – then bully bully. That was the creative idea.

- Creative thought is a **process** – the end goal being something of **tangible value**.

- Creative thought requires **conscious effort**. Those *EUREKA!* moments usually occur because you *make* them occur.

- Set the **physical stage** – create an environment that promotes creative thought.

- Set the **psychological stage** – create a *quiet mind*.

- **Define the problem** – you have to clearly understand what problem you are trying to solve.

- **Find the essence** – reduce the problem to its *intrinsic, indispensable,* and *crucial* properties.

- **Perform creative thought** – *it's a conscious act.*

- **Learn when to stop** – recognize when you've solved the problem.

- Implement your solution – **Get On With It** after you've solved the problem.

- And *have fun.*

Notes: